Free Verse Editions
Edited by Jon Thompson

Also by Molly Spencer

If the House

Hinge

Invitatory

Molly Spencer

Winner of the New Measure Poetry Prize

Parlor Press
Anderson, South Carolina
www.parlorpress.com

Parlor Press LLC, Anderson, South Carolina 29621

Library of Congress Cataloging-in-Publication Data on File

978-1-64317-433-4 (paperback)
978-1-64317-434-1 (pdf)
978-1-64317-435-8 (ePub)

1 2 3 4 5

Cover and interior design by David Blakesley
The painting on the cover is by Erin Lee Gafill, "Horizon, Blues." Used by permission.

Parlor Press LLC is an independent publisher of scholarly and trade titles in print and multimedia formats. This book is available in paperback and ebook formats from Parlor Press on the web at https://parlorpress.com or through online and brick-and-mortar bookstores. For submission information or to find out about Parlor Press publications, write to Parlor Press, 3015 Brackenberry Drive, Anderson, South Carolina 29621, or email editor@parlorpress.com.

For BP, AP, and LK—the reasons for my every *yes*.

The sea was one thing, once; the field another. Either way something got crossed or it didn't.

—Carl Phillips

You could live in that gap, that listening.

—Jorie Graham

Contents

//

//

//

//

Invitatory

Rowing, and Then Light

What's given me by the river, I'll leave to the river.

Islands of sky—flicker, the brim, and then light
on the tangled marsh.

Light where the cedars toppled

bone-like and silver. And later, hours of slow progress, swaying
marsh grass and the unrushed wandering of water,

the heron

unseen alongside, the heron
rising blue and somehow silent

though surely such unfolding has a song

or a cry—the heron lifting, the heron breaking
open into flight.

And who can I tell this to now—the children rowing on
ahead of me, the far west of you?

                              This is my account:
I didn't see the heron edgewise
then I saw it.

Wasn't rowing at all, only dipping the blade of my one oar
here, then there, to steer a little.

Let me drift, going nowhere, in the moment
the heron met my mind

though the moment was flawed and devoid
of meaning.

The cedars were not silver, not bone-like, the heron's flight
not soundless.

I'll speak of this to no one. The river bears me along.

//

Invitatory

Considering our momentary nearness

The planet we can't find but know is there
the size of ten Earths
because it pulls on everything

Field and edge of field
light and wing-bone, the far stones
of other moons

Something dropped in the night

Invitatory

Considering the moon's grip
on the snarled sea

The fraught raft
into which a father lowers
his child, a slender prayer

Shoreless
in his mouth—*have mercy*

The green untroubled heave of waves

Considering all the words for *gone*

What If I Wrote a Poem about Endings

Though it's true that once a window   opened
it would not be enough to say that once

a window opened
                   and the breeze seeped in

that, tenderly, you unpinned my hair.

                  In June, a ruin
of peonies all along the fence.

The Window | Nine Attempts

1.

I have returned to this
glass over miles

and through light
and time

the smell of dust
the body's salt

to tell you:
It still holds

the bones
of the swallow.

2.

It's true I have watched one red skiff   drift
reckless on the blue

                toward open water.

Have stood and marked the derelict moment
when distance won out over sight, the red skiff

lost now to the blue. True that *skiff* is a word
that suggests insignificance

which does not absolve me

of anything—not of caring more for seeing
than what's seen

nor my thirst for silence
which has formed
                a pane of glass in me.

A form to study light with. A genuine rescue.

3.

You said, notice what you're noticing. You said, ask yourself
what do I think about this, what do I think about that

all day long, ask yourself, what do I think.

I think there are days when the window lets in more sound than light.

I think I am at the window because it matters

what things are—river, wing-bone, girder, sill,
that *bird* once named the young of any kind

but does no longer. I think the window

is where time, in thinning light,
pours off the world like rain

off the eaves. Where I annotate
the days, the Earth's tilt

and spin, *not a world of objects but a world of events*—
I think we all might slip

away if this is true. I notice I am standing here naming
the hours and qualities of light

until the light fails.

4.

I think at the window
night expiring.

The thousandth shade of blue
light easterly. Death of

one moth, dust of its wing
on my fingertip not dissimilar

to the dust on the sill
I trace through saying *wrist*. I think

time and light keep happening
and happening. I think I see

ink-dark and shining
from the wing of one bird

one feather shed
on the walk

likely a primary
[that is, for flight]

numbered from
innermost to

outermost in keeping
with the molt pattern

wing with a notch
to augment lift

no longer. Forgive me
I think

the elegy
I stipulate

in this case is *vestige*
meaning *trace of*—a word

of unknown origin.
No, *mutable*

the cascading
derivatives of which refer

to the act of giving.
And taking.

5.

Or, to put it another way, here I am at the window again
where I have spent all day trying

to name the light. The light
which, like the stone, is granular. Where I have said,

it tumbles, *seeps through*, have hauled
these words in my arms over time and arid miles

only to set them down on the one line
that can hold them.

The line which, like light, is said to break.

Is said to be slant in certain hours.

6.

Then all day it shifts and lengthens, pools and stops short, pours itself out,
ripples like water over shoals,

like your fingertip
tracing down my keel.

I mean breastbone.

Lash and glower, billow and drift.

Next the light pulls and thickens—bands of mournful color at dusk
as if wounded by its own

diminishment. Then the dark seeps in,
the hours from all sides. I think

this is what I meant when I said: You are the night, deep and mineral,
not ungentle. When I said:

I am the body, hand on the wall, feeling my way through.

7.

I think the window happens
in the lisp of time and light.

Holds the separate consolations of the falling.
The searing night.

Tell me, is there a word for.
Is it time yet to.

I think the window happens
between shelter and glare

so that we can touch both
at the same time.

Here, where we are glass.

Annealed. Mended
but barely.

8.

I think I see the swallows singing
along the arched prayer

of flight. If not a world of objects, how does light
gild the very edge

of one wing? I notice the glass, reticent.
I think: Its distances

are thronging
in us. The scuffed horizon,

blue axiom
of longing.

The red skiff.
The red skiff

beyond sight. It is late
and I am not here

for half-measures,
nor to make amends.

9.

But which
window?

And Once Spoken Can a Thing Be Called Back

It was winter a long time
and then it was summer.
Then the sky

could hold only so much
until it had to fall
to its knees on the hillside

of you
as rain

as I have also done.

See, here is proof: the mark we made
on the earth—

the shape of me,
your pressed-down grasses.

Invitatory

Considering the pinprick
the needle carved from bone

Sliver in the heel sliver
in the curve of the heel fleeting
press of it in sand

Footprint at the water's edge

Footprint at the water's edge now stone

Invitatory

You ask me how I am

If I said sand in the spine of a book
If I said boneset common to your roadside

Early meadow rue desiring
damp shade at wood's edge

And stillness

Hanging its slow sepals down
petal-less
untouched

Sometimes called two houses

Notes on Confluence

1.

Some have nothing to do with rivers: Birches return first after disturbance.

That light is said to break where it enters
            water
                        or glass.

The indefinite continued progress of existence regarded
as a whole.

2.

Try to get something down

so I try *if*   I try *maybe*

glass and *wrist.*

Where two rivers meet and become one
      river.

Meander length: the lineal distance down-valley
                  where as a girl I loosened
my laces, left my shoes on the sand, a small trough

that carries water only
after rainfall.

3.

Entrain: incorporate and sweep along in its flow.
Entrain: cause another to fall

                                   into synchrony. *Even
          just a few words,* so I try *sediment.*

Which means
a sinking.
Means *descended tremblingly.*

I try *sink* but it comes out *skin.*

4.

Catchment: the catching or collecting of water
especially rainfall.

A reservoir or other
basin [in Latin, *pelvis*]

               where water collects.

[Here, inscribe in an image, a flicker
               of life   or time.]

Also, the water thus caught.

5.

The act of flowing together.
Left behind by flowing water.

Or to put it another way, here I am at the window again listening
for the sound of looking out and through

                                        as the curtains sail through light
       and time
                          which is a quiet sound, riverless. Alluvial, I try

once more *glass.*

I write it down but I can't see through it.

Lotic: having to do with flowing water.
Lentic: having to do with still.

6.

The place where two streams touch. A combined flood.

Or I did not foresee
        an entire city rising   here
in the place where your waters meet my waters.   I try

I will pull the stones of you.

I trace
the word *entire*

back to the word
untouched.

7.

Land through which runoff flows
                            to a single point in a stream: *watershed*.

Whether field or low marsh snowed over,
      I can't tell.

I try *I will pull the stones of you from my body*.

From my body painstakingly.

Leave them on the sand
                to dry and lose
      their markings, try instead *eddy*.

Which means *a circular movement
of water counter to a main current*.

Which means *again*,   *backwards*.

8.

It is written: *never the same river twice.*

It is written: *if you are coming down through the narrows.*

      This river distended, blue
in a basin—*tract of country drained by one river or draining into*
   one sea—of land as if holding itself

     back.
       And failing.

I try *small wavelets, crests glassy, no breaking.*

9.

This may have to do with wind and not rivers:

What If I Wrote a Poem about Time

And if you want the field defined, I'll show you
a window, west-facing   morning

wash of light through birches, shore-boned, overheard
thrum of boats threading
the long blue

          veer of afternoon,
a sandy two-track that leads to the water—

which is why
we need to talk about endings.

          You will be as far as the bridge

by year's end, you will be as far
as the bridge endlessly

and in blue.

Invitatory

In the night, three miles of land

Then lost again in the pooled blue
of a cloak draped over a corner chair

In the night, a woman bleeds through
a line on a map saying *hush*
to the child on her back

Or is that rain finally
in its thin voice

The sky kneeling down
in the fields at last
to glean

Invitatory

Once I stood in my kitchen and the Earth skipped
a beat, skidded, slipped

Then held
as the radio droned
the day's death count

As I browned the meat

Once another body formed in mine, raft adrift
on my waters

Her spine a primordial string
of stones stranded, curved shore of
alluvial things—how she lengthens now

Into the green of coming summer
easy sapling stride sunlit, backhand shadow of her
nearer to me now than her swung arms

As she walks on, a word
broken out of me

Trailing flesh and song

Poem Without Rivers

If the poplars that sail on the ridge are still
shaking their spangled hands,
if birches return first
after fire, and they do, bringing light
to the brink of the field,
if the lake's question in blue
is still a question—*What does one do*
with one's hands—then I
am walking through an astonishment
of dunes and this is a poem
about joy, in which
on the pier and gesturing
to the scuffed and silent distance, a mother
tells her children the oldest stories
the stories I told you, child,
from my deepest waters when
the orchards swooned heavy
with fruit in the clambering heat
of August, when I believed
I could make a word mean something
shore-like and actual: The mother
saved her children from the fire
by taking them to boundless waters,
Mama, the first word spoken,
nearly by accident, because the shape
of the mouth when pronouncing it
mimics the motion of feeding.
Saved them by crossing the lake.
She in her own body, they
in theirs, *swim*, she said, *swim*
with me. She is waiting for them
still, on a shore wind-built
hill of sand so broad and high
it's visible from space. Aeolian,

she waits. Looks out—
the blue rift, the dark curves
etched on the waters—
the Manitous, which the story says
are her children, still swimming,
but are mere islands.
Waits as another year lists
like a swamped boat
toward winter and amid
a long cycle of erosion
which means *a gnawing
away*, knowing now which life
the poet meant when she wrote
the only life you could save.

Of Wind, or Air

Of vessels

The last bowl in her hands in the final kitchen.

Through the window, shore then sea, on its rim a ship
imperceptibly crossing.

If you think you can hear anything in this wind.

And swallows slice the blue.
And sand seethes the hours by, the sea scrapes in and out like a terrible door.

And once spoken can a thing be called back.

The ship still crossing. The swallows slicing, swooping.

If you think you can hear anything.

The white bowl not yet falling, the window holding everything.

Lexical

It is said the swallow has more air in its bones than other birds.

I am unable to verify this but can tell you a wing is a paired appendage,
a feather is a dead thing.

So the wind spills over the primaries, the secondaries, so the coverts cover.

So the swallows lift, so they swoop.

The bowl, which was said to have *nested*.
Her at the window not singing.

Where the wing fastens to the chest, where breastplate and breath, where the wing endeavors

toward the heart, nearly touches, where bone
nestles into bone at last,

this we call *articulation*.

Which means *a joining*.

Which also means *a division into distinct parts*.

If the wing is said to be *pinioned* there.
And it is said to be pinioned there.

If *pinion* means *to tie or hold the arms and legs*, if it means *to cut a wing in order to
        disable it*.
And it does.

And once spoken can a thing be called back.

If with these words we speak of flight.

Of flight

How a wing works: the wind falls
on a concave surface.

How flight began: from the trees down, from the ground up.

The birds have lost their expendable bones
and those that remain are hollow.

Like the house on the hillside
of memory is hollow.

Like the last bowl in her hands,
the arid, untouched body—what once was a hand

is now the mere trace of a hand.
The word for this: *vestigial.*

If you think you can hear anything in this wind.

Drag: the backward-reaching pull of air along a flying thing.
Drag: the inherent cost of the wing.

Ligature

How to *un-* that thready '&' they made,
never-rhymed.

If he had raveled through
her like breath.

If nest instead of dune gnawed away by the mouth
of the wind.

If the final bowl had held in the trace
of her hands.

And once spoken can a thing be called back.

If there were a word that meant *something used to tie or bind tightly*.
And there is.

If the same word also meant *thread or cord to tie off a bleeding*.

Of contronyms

Dismember means *to take a way a limb.*

I want one word for *wrist*, one for its underside,
fluvial and threaded in blue.

And *ravel* means *a tangle*
and *to un-
tangle.*

If you think you can hear anything in this wind.

The bowl—if she undropped it, if it had held like bridges hold
trembling, as a blown nest holds
in the wind

because it is anchored.

And if *anchor*
first meant
to bend.

Would *skin* still mean *a thin layer of tissue forming the outer cover
of the body.* Would it still mean *to scratch, scrape, or peel the skin off.*

Is there a word that can hold the world still—
eminence maybe, maybe *skein*, a word that can make a crossing ship

stop crossing.
Make a ship endlessly crossing to have crossed.

And once spoken can a thing be called back.

I say *splice*
so as not to say *we are come between.*

I say *splice*
so as not to say *grafted upon you.*

Nor can you leave it to the birds

Of the set of nested bowls, none remains.

This is a word: *lossless. Lingual* is a word
meaning *having to do with the tongue.*

The tongue which is richly supplied with blood.
The tongue which is said to have a blade.

She who thought she would remember
does not remember

the vessel breaking, the last white bowl
                                        slipping

from her hands

                    five small bones of the swallow's tongue.

And once spoken can a thing be called back.

Her on her knees sweeping.

Kite

A heavier-than-air craft with wing surfaces.

A medium-to-large bird of prey fond of updrafts.

[If you think you can hear anything in this wind.]

Also meaning *fly, move quickly,*

                    likely imitative of a bird's cry.

Invitatory

Considering all the words for gone
cities whose lights flared rough
on the crust—

Carthage, salt-sown
Eišiškės and its thousand useless shoes

City of every house
in which one woman kneads the bread
in the half-dawn with the brief birds

Of her hands, city of the bridge that held
city of the bridge that fell

Low-skied city in which you loved me

Each touch roaming
my spare rooms, city where

The toll of the bell
split the bell

Where still its knell

Enters the sleep of the living

Invitatory

Considering all we know of skin
sky and ruin

Still the path of any body
toward another is thorned-over and trackless

The female dragonfly faking her death
to evade male advances

Penelope at her loom
Odysseus stuck in traffic on the 101

The word *eclipse*
which means *abandonment*
and after

All of us walking together
and alone down the unlit

Slope of the newest night

What If I Wrote a Poem about Joy

And the field alongside and brooding,

the chicory another blue
            astonishment
    in the summer-long ditch—

Close your eyes
as you held me.

Where years from now the deer lies down
for the last time

        and the highway's clear all the way
to the bridge—   *Close them again.*

And we were.

Invitatory

And could we make of this a home—
the oldest known woven garment

Could we ask how long
did you linen her bones in the tomb
before your pleats ebbed

Before your sleeves unsleeved
and what sound was made
in the unsleeving

Was it a slack sound and silken

Not a rending but a body slipping
from a room

Not latch-click but hand
unfastening

Knot-slip, hair let down at last, not sleeve at all

But the quiet
ulna
that outlasts it

The Uses of Distance

And then what I wanted was to watch the bones soften in snow.

Watch the snow gather in folds along the bones, the bones in the ditch where the deer lay down, the ones I've mentioned before. And the birches, too, alongside and bare-limbed as if chiseled. Bright against the sky.

A stalled sky, fathomless gray and snow falling, the birches like hindsight, the delicate harp of the bones in the ditch.

And always the field

Of the mind's eye or of memory, the field patient and bounded, empty room of the earth—it fills, and this is distance. Or this is a room to dwell in.

Either one, I am crossing.

Either one, I am on my way to you.

//

Or it could go like this: I watched the ship on the horizon, watched it cross the field of my vision

Imperceptibly. It was morning, low tide and gull-cry, breeze and blade of light, blue and blue hovering, two blues brush-stroked, blurred and notional, a line where faintly a ship was crossing and not crossing.

No inland house to return to, as if having chosen.

Light at my back, press of bare hours. The wind's contours sanding the earth, most remote province of the sea seen from shore.

Or nearer, the rib, the space between ribs, *interstitial* is the word, ridge of light along the body's last edge—

We call it *skin*.

What I mean is that I believed the ship to be crossing though it did not appear to be crossing, and that this should mean something indelible and whole, the field unbidden but crossable.

Believed you to be elsewhere but palpable, a harp string plucked. An aftermath.

Somewhere, the field mown down. Blade for the first time.

//

That's because you said you wanted more silence
you said.

And it's true, I did say I wanted that: trees reticent in their shade, fugitive light along this limb and that limb, the verdant deep

Of a room where two can be together and, though nothing is spoken, all is said, my thatched field laid down beneath your galloping skies.

Room of no wind, where a finger traced along a wrist, or the sill, or a river writes an ending.

Room that cloaks itself in a blue I can walk through. And you will be there and not there standing at a window, a sea

With its edge far and notional, reciting a blue distance. You, wary and dusk-etched, looking out, your back to me, string of a harp unplucked. The light doorless and un-claimed, another day irrevocable.

And the silence comes again. And the silence holds
what the body holds no longer.

//

As if I could speak of a river and have it mean only *river*. As if *river* did not once mean the land alongside, as if *river* will not once again crest in the night, tide wandered inland.

As if every heart were not a levee about to breach or collapse.

Now that we know the bridge we thought would hold instead has fallen.

Now that every word tastes of salt and time passing, hours turned loose, skein of light unraveling along a surface, a sill.

A wrist.

Or every word instead tastes of rust, trouble and song, light now touching, love, the curve of your neck where it softens into shoulder. Where my hands and head have rested. As if given the word *river*

A knot loosens and this we call *current* which means *to run*.

Or once again, the birds have flocked, a hundred dark hands in the one oak, edge of the field.

Once again, the field incessant.

//

Slant of dusk as muted, swung. Window-glass, blue-hearted.

Or that's what you said when you spoke of me—*you are glass* and the glass of you blue-hearted, many-windowed body blue at dusk, and memory falls

All night in the petals of the flowering trees dappling the walk by morning. Memory shed and dented. Thin-skinned.

Or past the city's final streets there was a field, folded and flightless.

Or there was a forest and a forest

Was for entering. What I want to know is what we've made here, one shade of blue or more. Your blue at my waking, bruised miles, the thronging blue architectures of time.

Love, leave the window open to the wind and rain, the rain we have waited for, the rain supple and insistent. Its utterance. Listen.

It is falling on the bruised petals strewn along the walk, falling into the threshed and endless handfuls of water in the river, the grinding sea, falling on the roof above this room in a city that is not lost to us, a city where we are the petals and the blue and the rain.

Where we are aftermath. Where after everything

We have laid down in the just-mown field of one another.

//

Light that skims the field all day.

Light—as if to hold it.

Or in your hands, held, I was clay, elemental. Light gilding river here, sea there, margin of light blurred at its edge, blue and notional.

As if to call the field *clearing, made place*, once, long ago, warm shallow sea. As if to have to choose field over river, river over sea, blue, the bridges at night, at dawn, a window.

As if standing in the glassy rift we call longing.

And now I know myself to be the rain falling on your city, silk strap slipping off a shoulder, night gliding off beneath the bridge past where light gives way to blue then deeper blue.

Now that each blue has its own name. Bridges and piers of bridges, wind and song of wind.

As if I could not also say *field's edge, vestige, ditch* where the deer lay down, tentative harp of bones. Tell me

What is field and what is wilderness.

I mean tenderness.

Is it a forest, does it darken all night in your chest, is the wind green and soughing through us, is that rain again.

Am I half-built.

Am I ruin.

//

As if I could keep saying *field* and have it mean only *field*, as if grasses after grasses after grasses could mean *sea*. Skim of

One hand along wild blooms cresting in the wind that holds the storm off, in the wind that hauls the storm across the ridge.

And if you could, would you cross it, would your body halve the green, would you wade toward me in a field of light and lost things, teeming and rooted, hillside aching gold. Try

To describe a crossing thing and a thing crossing, try saying *distance* and have not mean *to stand apart*,

As if longing were not just a sea of grasses recalling its first August, wanting rest, wanting, in fact, the blade.

As if our bodies were not small boats, drifting though moored, as if the bridge were not hours from here. Days. Light-years.

As if the field could not roll like a sea in strong wind and close the distance between us.

//

And if I stay, I'll speak only the quiet words.

Wrist and *linen*   *swallows*   *breezeway*   *wingless*   *want*

If the earth tilts again toward its coldnesses, and it will—

The coming reliable snows, morning so hushed one might never hear the sun as it seeps through the trees, which are behind me. As it pours light into all cities and all fields, which are behind me.

If all rivers.

And when edges.

And is *bridge* a quiet word, is *windless*, field mown down, green and green and waiting for light. If *to be filled* is the same as *to relent*.

And if you walk, whether through or alongside, is this aftermath, if you dream of losing your way, if it's colder where you are than before

And late now. If the days are thinning in the bony hands of time, am I a field

Tilled under, have I folded myself over for you as a means of shoring up, would we otherwise fail or decline.

If I could go but have not gone.

And is *wait* a quiet word. Is *crossing*.

//

So that when the flowering trees flowered that year, I knew them to be both bloom and ash.

So that when the wind poured through their limbs at night they became an archive of touch, words you said to me   *unreadable   balcony   thicket   blue—*

And the bridges reach for shores, tremble imperceptibly as a means of not falling

And this, too, is distance.

Or this is: In the borrowed city, I cannot have the many-streeted darkness, the glint of light falling from a window, I cannot have the lush beloved

Mosses softening the steps.

Your wrist, its underside in the layered dark. A lantern. A song. The river's endless blue glide. Longing set loose in me, *the portions of the bridge still standing after the collapse.*

And the section of the bridge underwater and given, a dimness in me your hands can't reach. Skin or silk, silt, nearly silent though given what's fallen.

Though given what's fallen waters rise.

//

Until, like the birches, I learn to bend and sway in the unsaid

Wind of your name, or until the field, like all fields, holds me greening.

And when time and weather, when silence, make a song of the bones of the one deer fallen.

Until grasses.

Or when summer.

And if alongside a thicket of birches, and then field of. Grasses, ditch at the road's edge, bones picked bare at last.

In August's last chord. You said, *think of beginnings and middles*.

Until, like the birches, I recur after fire, spread my seed in a cold season.

Until solace.

And when birdsong

Alone, or if a glassy absence is what we hear most.

Until light returns. Until snow covers all.

The bones in the ditch where the deer lay down.

You said, *the end is not yet written*.

Until next year's grasses, brooding, reliable, beneath.

//

Not the field itself but the field's quiet

Contentment and the stars, but only after the smoke clears from the night sky where the road gestures toward its northernmosts. Where the road swerves for the tree cut down years ago now

And this is lostness or merely loss, the gaps, light spilling, *interstitial*. Blanks between birches, blanks between bones, every chink or delay. The bridges. Song torn free of the throat of the bird. What is the word for *the wind*

Comes roaming endlessly and in blue. What are the true things—salt, skin, field of light though it is waning, the patient ribs of the deer, love maybe—

That wingéd thing circling the blown field on updrafts almost bringing us back to each other.

Not reticence. Not the patient stand of birches, but the way the snows unmade the path to them by morning.

//

So that after, there was a new kind of quiet.

Not the quiet of winter but the quiet of wind swallowing lesser sounds, quiet of glass seen through. So that we could see

The ship crossing the horizon and know its engine churned but not hear the churning. So that we knew the swallows, as if ash, sang, but did not hear their song.

And the tapering of daylight was not lost on us.

Not lost on us: the curtain's *shush* along the floor.

So that when our bodies' borders blurred there was a name for it   *estuary plucked string   bridge* or *bridge of glass.*

Not the floor beneath you now but the floor you crossed to touch me.

And the swallows swung and swooped as if songless and not site-faithful. And the site of this new quiet was inland and hovering, blue and blue through a window.

Not the window where I'm standing now but the window of the room inside the body. Where all along the ship that had crossed was the ship that was crossing.

The inmost room called the *keep.*

A spill of light that says at last, *come in.*

//

There's no such thing as half-a-trespass, a little bit dead, in the ditch where the deer lay down for the last time, and the birches alongside, knowing north is north, knowing the light's at my back, the rest is memory, lostness, rivers, blue.

Even if the year keeps folding over into winter, even if you're still gone and I'm still here drifting loose

Along the ditch where the deer lay down, the terminal bones, *the image and the alteration.*

And the field or the distance or the room fills, and the ship has crossed or is yet crossing, the river crawls away in black. And the road out again—what is it to want, anyway?—the road out, ribboning, unsolved, the snow palpable

Where a hand has plucked a string to make a song. Desire.

The birches, that delicate harp of bones in the ditch, not softer but sharper.

I came here to see if the field is still a field.

And Once Spoken Can a Thing Be Called Back

The shortest distance between two points—
city and outskirts

headwaters of a river and
mouth of a river

field and ditch at the edge of—

by which I mean
touch me.

Invitatory

Three times, I have felt the downward twisting pull
of a child

The downward twisting pull of a child wanting

Three times, I have felt the downward twisting
pull of a child wanting rough earth
after months of calm sea

My heart and

My heart and the supple cage

Three times, my heart and the supple cage
of my body—shell split

Open
fed upon

Left at the strandline

Invitatory

And the floods drape over fields and lifetimes, end of winter

And the gunman kills fifty at prayer while we sleep

And here, beneath this latest and most tenuous roof,
I am eyeing the door

I am abandoning them slowly—
their delible skin, their six blue eyes in all

What I mean is that their cries tug at my ribs
only loosely now

That my eyes are cast far off

Now, thirty-nine found dead in a refrigerated truck

A child in a cage, a thousand-thousand children
in a thousand-thousand cages, this is the world

I brought them to by way of my own bleak body,
ladder of

World of stone and churning
waters, fire at the rim, shackle and hunger, each bridge a bridge a-tremble

Only world I had to give: swerve in the road where the tree once stood

And this is time and time passing, all those times
I looked at them in the rearview, said, *no more questions for a while*

By now they must know
there is a bird who lays her eggs
in another bird's nest

Then flies off to follow her hunger

And Once Spoken Can a Thing Be Called Back

What if winter again gives way and the field

                                        again rears up in green

          and profusion.

If the wind
riffles one wing on the roadside

                was the wing never paired.

What if the field is not a distance
but a tenderness

between us—a last-year's leaf caught
in the chicory
          blooming.

Meuse

Not a quiet place, she wrote, *but a place
in a long period of quiet.*

//

You were never wrong about the blue—that blue
denotes distance, I mean.

I mean how the ocean seemed both to hover
and to tend.

How the horizon hung above itself and the crossing
        ship both crossed and seemed

never to cross.

//

I mean once the girl when small
                        held the pale star

of her hand just above the grass and said, *the sky
    where the birds live starts right here.*

//

Skies and birds and the words we give to birdsong:
drop it   drop it   cover it up.

//

And blue is only blue because the light gets lost.
And the terrible waiting fault has not yet slipped.

And where you lay down, I was a sudden downhill clearing   I was
the field and a tenuous theory

                              of the field
pressed into your shape   by your body.

//

And the small girl marking the sky with her hand
became the small girl whose breath leaked

away, the girl who went blue as I held her.

//

Once a window and once a breeze
              nuzzling the sheers asway, a stack of books in the window,
fore-edges facing the street.

//

What I mean is that our word for *able to be touched*
                 or felt began on the strings of a harp,

a fingertip's tug that made distance into song.

//

That is, a particular rib is said to be *floating*,
a joint can be a *birdsmouth*.

A wind called *mistral*, a wind called *gale*.

Wreckhouse, zephyr, capsize, chord—
many and various names for wind.

//

The girl,
            the one whose breezes
stilled as the air stills before storm—
                          torn petal of her.

And the fault—I have tread upon it in the drift that is
my body   and it let me,

it held.

//

Sheers a-sway or were those bodies   barely seen
summer's dust and clinging

to each other as if to a raft in the unsoundable blue.

//

The small girl gone
blue—they brought her back to me

pink and crying, they brought her back

                        to me, faint morning
            breezes, her legible wind.

//

How we trembled there, as if petals.

I mean at the edge of
where bodies fold
into the blue.

//

When the fault slips, it will not be a breaking apart.
It will not be a scraping alongside.   It will be a folding into, a plunge and crumple.

          Then a final, terrible rinsing   away.

Tell me that after, you will open a door and enter
       again the room where the breeze plucks

your body, plangent   where once   we stood rib against rib

       in the window.

//

And the small girl did not die though the harp sang
and sang three times. Though the harp sang
and sang three times the small girl did not die.

//

Room where light still gathers
in the corners of your eyes.

//

What I mean is I have followed words along their skittish paths toward the stranded
drift
        of margins.   I have remembered you

there, where words founder into silence, blue of fading
        harp song, where the sea is still blue
                                and the ship is still crossing.

//

[Quiver of]

//

        A stack of books   in the window,
fore-edges facing the street

as I pass by.

//

What I mean is: I have made of my body a hillside,
lie down. What I mean

                is: Once we had a word for *the form of an animal left by its lying*.

What If I Wrote a Love Poem

Winter always begins
at the shoreline

where one coldness turns
to touch another coldness

and clings. Touch
                    touch

again—present tense and
irrevocable.

//

Invitatory

You ask me is this a road, what does dust mean

You say there are distances there are a thousand words
for blue there are no lamps in the windows you say

Every room in the house except this one

The empty balconies, you say, of your body, the pliant line
of light along your wrist

Its underside
you say
then are quiet

The road considers its ongoingness

Amaranth: 'unfading'

The one bridge ceded to us ceded to us still

I have turned off the porch light to give you cover,
have you kept the stone I put in your hand

And Once Spoken Can a Thing Be Called Back

Now that we know a bird's song is distinct from its call—
        the swallow's song guttural, its call a soft *chur.*

Now that we know one is for desire, one for the ordinary—
        await what the stars bring, row of threads on a loom.

Having hauled the whole, blue downslur of my warble
        behind me for a thousand-thousand miles to the edge

Of you once more.

And If an Essential Thing Has Flown Between Us

Quiver of
the three little bones

of the ear
struck with birdsong.

Here I am right near you.
Low, even croaking

in flight.

Invitatory

You ask me are you happy

Mornings, I read and get some words down
as I have always done

Sundays, I fill the lamps with oil—
another week's light

Though quiet, I am not indifferent

Not seen-through, not shore
awaiting

I parse again this distance, light
on a slow river

I have not forgotten

How tenderly
you unpinned
my hair

A Defense

All night I hear the river asking
to cross me and I say, *fine, cross me.*

I won't deny the downstream waters that run through me,
the sediment, or the light that shreds as the current weaves.

So, yes, I will wade out past the shallows.
I will walk into the rusted blade of the river,
which resists me, and go essentially nowhere.

Let me say it, then, that I am stone. And have tired.

That I have woken in a glittering, spring-fed cold
and called it *cold.*

See how the river has smoothed my coarse edges, dragging me along
then unhanding me to settle in its bed, veined and woven.

I am not sorry to rest here amid
the alluvial, colorful hardnesses.

Invitatory

Dawn again and the birds of oblivion sing
of all hungers

Each day I wake
to a pillar of light kindling the room
into being once more

A crease in the rug, someone's future stumble

The pale melt of bedclothes at my thighs

Mine is not the face of peace but of the found-out

The lamp's diminutive thorn
of light sharpens at my bedside—
a whole world waiting

Again
for my *yes*

Notes

The epigraphs to the collection are from Carl Phillips's poem "Brothers in Arms" and Jorie Graham's poem "Eschatological Prayer."

Unless otherwise noted, etymological information and definitions are from *Barnhart's Concise Dictionary of Etymology*, or *Etymonline*; all river- and water-related terms and definitions are from the Texas River Guide's online *Glossary of River Terminology*; bird-song mnemonics are from "Mnemonic Bird Songs," by South Bay Birders Unlimited.

"The Window| Nine Attempts": In section two, "A form to study light with. A genuine rescue." is a reference to Robert Frost's explanation of form in art: "What are the ideals of form for if we aren't going to be made to fear them? All our ingenuity is lavished on getting into danger legitimately so that we may be genuinely rescued." In section three, *"not a world of objects but a world of events"* is from Carlos Rovelli's *Reality Is Not What It Seems: The Journey to Quantum Gravity.*

"Notes on Confluence": In section one, the phrase *"the indefinite continued progress of existence regarded as a whole"* is an abbreviated version of the *Concise Oxford English Dictionary* definition of the word *time*. In the section three, "descended tremblingly" is from Walt Whitman's "Song of Myself," Part 11. In section seven *"a circular movement of water counter to a main current"* is from the Apple dictionary, version 2.3.0 (268). In section eight, "never the same river twice" is Heraklitus; "if you are coming down through the narrows" is from Ezra Pound's translation of Li Bai's "The River Merchant's Wife: A Letter"; *"small wavelets, crests glassy, no breaking"* is from the Beaufort Wind Scale.

"What If I Wrote a Poem About Time": The poem begins with a borrowing from Lia Purpura's poetry collection, *King Baby*. Her lines are "If you want a field defined / I'll show you a field."

"Poem Without Rivers": The last line is a paraphrase of the last two lines of Mary Oliver's poem "The Journey," which read "the only life that you could / save."

"Of Wind, or Air": The structure and sectioning of this poem is indebted to Carolina Ebeid's poem, "Veronicas of a Matador." In "Contronym," the phrase "we are come between" is from Charles Wright's poem "Homage to Paul Cezanne." The subtitle *"Nor can you leave it to the birds*" is a line from Venus Khoury-Ghata's "Internments," translated by Marilyn Hacker.

"The Uses of Distance": In "[Light that skims the field all day]" "*made place*" is from Robert Duncan's poem "Often I am Permitted to Return to a Meadow." In "[So that when the flowering trees blossomed]," the italicized text is from the Wikipedia entry on the Tacoma Narrows Bridge, which collapsed in strong winds a few months after its completion in 1940. In "[There's no such thing as half-a-trespass]," the phrase "the image and the alteration" is from Barbara Guest's poem "Alteration"; Guest's lines are: "I ask you to permit the image // and the alteration of time."

"Meuse": The italicized lines in the first stanza are from Kathryn Schulz's article "The Really Big One," *The New Yorker*, July 13, 2015. The italicized line at the end of the poem, which comprises the definition of *meuse*, is C.D. Wright's.

"And Once Spoken Can a Thing Be Called Back [Now that we know a bird's song is distinct from its call]": The italicized lines are from etymological definitions of the words "desire" and "ordinary."

"And If an Essential Thing Has Flown Between Us": The title is a line from Muriel Rukeyser's poem "Sonnet."

Acknowledgments

Sincere thanks to the editors and staff of the journals who first published these poems, sometimes in different versions and under different titles:

Los Angeles Review: "Rowing, and Then Light"; "The Uses of Distance [So that after there was a new kind of quiet.]"
On the Seawall: "The Window | Nine Attempts"
Prairie Schooner: "A Defense"
Poetry Northwest: "Notes on Confluence"

//

"A Defense," under the title "Fluvial," received a Glenna Luschei Award from *Prairie Schooner*.

//

Deep gratitude to the earliest readers of this manuscript whose thoughtful feedback and questions helped me to understand what the work was and how to bring it into a final form: David Biespiel and Joy Manesiotis. Thanks, too, to David Roderick for his thoughtful reading and feedback on a later version of the manuscript.

Thank you to Erin Lee Gafill for allowing me to use an image of her painting "Horizon, Blues" as cover art.

//

And fathomless thanks to these dear friends in poetry, whose company I treasure in this life of reading, writing, and mothering: Jennifer Richter, Kelly Cressio-Moeller, Sally Rosen Kindred, Sandy Longhorn, Lena Khalaf Tuffaha, Cate Hodorowicz, Billie Swift, Amanda Moore, Marisa Siegel, and, again, Joy Manesiotis.

About the Author

Molly Spencer is a poet, critic, essayist, and editor. Her debut collection, *If the House* (2019), won the Brittingham Prize judged by Carl Phillips. A second collection, *Hinge* (2020) won the Crab Orchard Open Competition judged by Allison Joseph. Molly's poetry has appeared in *Blackbird, FIELD, New England Review, Ploughshares, Prairie Schooner*, and other journals. Her critical writing and essays have appeared at *The Georgia Review, Kenyon Review, Literary Hub, The Writer's Chronicle*, and *The Rumpus*, where she is a senior poetry editor. Spencer's work has been awarded the Lucile Medwick Memorial Award from the Poetry Society of America, a Glenna Luschei Award from *Prairie Schooner*, and an Institute for the Humanities Faculty Fellowship at the University of Michigan, where she teaches writing at the Gerald R. Ford School of Public Policy.

Photograph of the author by Focal Point Studios. Used by permission.

Free Verse Editions

Edited by Jon Thompson

13 ways of happily by Emily Carr
& in Open, Marvel by Felicia Zamora
& there's you still thrill hour of the world to love by Aby Kaupang
Alias by Eric Pankey
the atmosphere is not a perfume it is odorless by Matthew Cooperman
At Your Feet (A Teus Pés) by Ana Cristina César, edited by Katrina Dodson, trans. by Brenda Hillman and Helen Hillman
Bari's Love Song by Kang Eun-Gyo, translated by Chung Eun-Gwi
Between the Twilight and the Sky by Jennie Neighbors
Blood Orbits by Ger Killeen
The Bodies by Christopher Sindt
The Book of Isaac by Aidan Semmens
The Calling by Bruce Bond
Canticle of the Night Path by Jennifer Atkinson
Child in the Road by Cindy Savett
Civil Twilight by Giles Goodland
Condominium of the Flesh by Valerio Magrelli, trans. by Clarissa Botsford
Contrapuntal by Christopher Kondrich
Country Album by James Capozzi
Cry Baby Mystic by Daniel Tiffany
The Curiosities by Brittany Perham
Current by Lisa Fishman
Day In, Day Out by Simon Smith
Dear Reader by Bruce Bond
Dismantling the Angel by Eric Pankey
Divination Machine by F. Daniel Rzicznek
Elsewhere, That Small by Monica Berlin
Empire by Tracy Zeman
Erros by Morgan Lucas Schuldt
Extinction of the Holy City by Bronisław Maj, trans. by Daniel Bourne
Fifteen Seconds without Sorrow by Shim Bo-Seon, trans. by Chung Eun-Gwi and Brother Anthony of Taizé
The Forever Notes by Ethel Rackin
The Flying House by Dawn-Michelle Baude
General Release from the Beginning of the World by Donna Spruijt-Metz

Ghost Letters by Baba Badji

Go On by Ethel Rackin

Here City by Rick Snyder

An Image Not a Book by Kylan Rice

Instances: Selected Poems by Jeongrye Choi, trans. by Brenda Hillman, Wayne de Fremery, & Jeongrye Choi

Invitatory by Molly Spencer

Last Morning by Simon Smith

The Magnetic Brackets by Jesús Losada, trans. by M. Smith & L. Ingelmo

Man Praying by Donald Platt

A Map of Faring by Peter Riley

The Miraculous Courageous by Josh Booton

Mirrorforms by Peter Kline

A Myth of Ariadne by Martha Ronk

No Shape Bends the River So Long by Monica Berlin & Beth Marzoni

North | Rock | Edge by Susan Tichy

Not into the Blossoms and Not into the Air by Elizabeth Jacobson

Overyellow, by Nicolas Pesquès, translated by Cole Swensen

Parallel Resting Places by Laura Wetherington

pH of Au by Vanessa Couto Johnson

Physis by Nicolas Pesquès, translated by Cole Swensen

Pilgrimage Suites by Derek Gromadzki

Pilgrimly by Siobhán Scarry

Poems from above the Hill & Selected Work by Ashur Etwebi, trans. by Brenda Hillman & Diallah Haidar

The Prison Poems by Miguel Hernández, trans. by Michael Smith

Puppet Wardrobe by Daniel Tiffany

Quarry by Carolyn Guinzio

remanence by Boyer Rickel

Republic of Song by Kelvin Corcoran

Rumor by Elizabeth Robinson

Settlers by F. Daniel Rzicznek

A Short History of Anger by Joy Manesiotis

Signs Following by Ger Killeen

Small Sillion by Joshua McKinney

Split the Crow by Sarah Sousa

Spine by Carolyn Guinzio

Spool by Matthew Cooperman

Strange Antlers by Richard Jarrette

A Suit of Paper Feathers by Nate Duke
Summoned by Guillevic, trans. by Monique Chefdor & Stella Harvey
Sunshine Wound by L. S. Klatt
System and Population by Christopher Sindt
These Beautiful Limits by Thomas Lisk
They Who Saw the Deep by Geraldine Monk
The Thinking Eye by Jennifer Atkinson
This History That Just Happened by Hannah Craig
An Unchanging Blue: Selected Poems 1962–1975 by Rolf Dieter Brinkmann, trans. by Mark Terrill
Under the Quick by Molly Bendall
Verge by Morgan Lucas Schuldt
The Visible Woman by Allison Funk
The Wash by Adam Clay
Well by Sasha Steensen
We'll See by Georges Godeau, trans. by Kathleen McGookey
What Stillness Illuminated by Yermiyahu Ahron Taub
Winter Journey [Viaggio d'inverno] by Attilio Bertolucci, trans. by Nicholas Benson
Wonder Rooms by Allison Funk

Printed in the USA
CPSIA information can be obtained
at www.ICGtesting.com
JSHW072022270924
70524JS00008B/20